First Steps to Numbe

Book 3

Contents

Folens Publishers

Add on the number lines.

Put your finger on **1**. Count on **2** more.

0 – 1 – 2 – 3 – 4 – 5 – 6 – 7 – 8 – 9 – 10

1 + 2 = 3

Put your finger on **2**. Count on **4** more.

0 – 1 – 2 – 3 – 4 – 5 – 6 – 7 – 8 – 9 – 10

2 + 4 = ☐

Put your finger on **4**. Count on **6** more.

0 – 1 – 2 – 3 – 4 – 5 – 6 – 7 – 8 – 9 – 10

4 + 6 = ☐

Add

3 + 5 = ☐ **2 + 7 = ☐**

Write the sums shown on the number lines.

4 + 3 = [7]

__ + __ = [ ]

__ + __ = [ ]

__ + __ = [ ]

Write the missing number on each shirt.

Colour **5**.

Colour **4**.

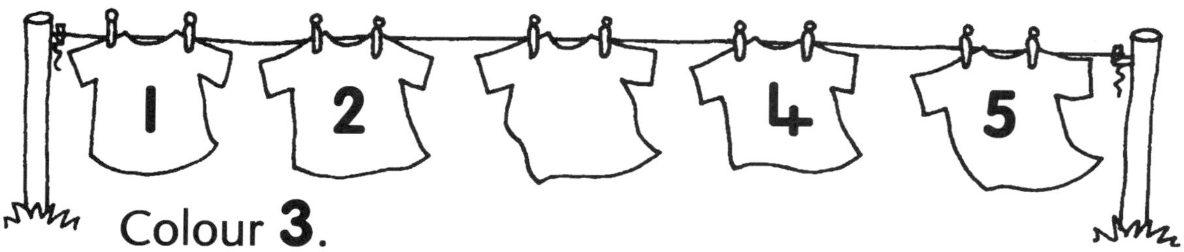

Colour **3**.

Colour **2**.

Colour **1**.

The story of 2.

1	**2**	3	4	5	6	7	8	9	10

2 + 0 = 2

1 + 1 = 2

0 + 2 = 2

2 + 0 = ☐

1 + 1 = ☐

0 + 2 = ☐

2 is **1** more than ☐

2 is **1** less than ☐

Add **2.** 

 add  equals **5**

3 + 2 = **5**

+ 2

1	3
2	6
3	4
4	5
5	7

+ 2

1	→	3
2	→	
3	→	
4	→	
5	→	

2 2 2 2 2 2

2 2 2 2 2 2

Add.

●   ●●   ●●●

$1 + 2 = 3$ or $\begin{array}{r} 1 \\ +\,2 \\ \hline 3 \\ \hline \end{array}$

$\begin{array}{r} 1 \\ +\,2 \\ \hline \\ \hline \end{array}$ $\begin{array}{r} 2 \\ +\,2 \\ \hline \\ \hline \end{array}$ $\begin{array}{r} 3 \\ +\,2 \\ \hline \\ \hline \end{array}$ $\begin{array}{r} 4 \\ +\,2 \\ \hline \\ \hline \end{array}$

$\begin{array}{r} 2 \\ +\,4 \\ \hline \\ \hline \end{array}$ $\begin{array}{r} 2 \\ +\,3 \\ \hline \\ \hline \end{array}$ $\begin{array}{r} 2 \\ +\,2 \\ \hline \\ \hline \end{array}$ $\begin{array}{r} 2 \\ +\,1 \\ \hline \\ \hline \end{array}$

$1 + 1 =$ ☐ $2 + 0 + 0 =$ ☐

$0 + 1 + 1 =$ ☐ $0 + 2 + 0 =$ ☐

$1 + 0 + 1 =$ ☐ $1 + 0 + 0 =$ ☐

The story of **3**.

0	1	2	**3**	4	5	6	7	8	9	10

3

3 + 0 = 3

2 + 1 = 3

3

1 + 2 = 3

0 + 3 = 3

3

3 + 0 =	☐	**1 + 2 =**	☐
2 + 1 =	☐	**0 + 3 =**	☐

3

3 is **1** more than ☐

3 is **1** less than ☐

Add **3**. 

 add  equals **6**

3 + 3 = 6

+ 3

1	5
2	6
3	7
4	8
5	4

+ 3

1	→	4
2	→	
3	→	
4	→	
5	→	

3 3 3 3 3 3

3 3 3 3 3 3

Add.

● ●●● ●●●●

$1 + 3 = 4$ or $\begin{array}{r} 1 \\ +3 \\ \hline 4 \\ \hline \end{array}$

$\begin{array}{r} 1 \\ +3 \\ \hline \\ \hline \end{array}$ $\begin{array}{r} 2 \\ +3 \\ \hline \\ \hline \end{array}$ $\begin{array}{r} 3 \\ +3 \\ \hline \\ \hline \end{array}$ $\begin{array}{r} 4 \\ +3 \\ \hline \\ \hline \end{array}$

$\begin{array}{r} 5 \\ +3 \\ \hline \\ \hline \end{array}$ $\begin{array}{r} 6 \\ +3 \\ \hline \\ \hline \end{array}$ $\begin{array}{r} 7 \\ +3 \\ \hline \\ \hline \end{array}$ $\begin{array}{r} 3 \\ +1 \\ \hline \\ \hline \end{array}$

$\begin{array}{r} 3 \\ +2 \\ \hline \\ \hline \end{array}$ $\begin{array}{r} 3 \\ +5 \\ \hline \\ \hline \end{array}$

$1 + 1 + 1 = \square$ $2 + 1 + 0 = \square$

$2 + 0 + 1 = \square$ $0 + 2 + 1 = \square$

$0 + 1 + 2 = \square$ $0 + 3 + 0 = \square$

The story of 4.

0	1	2	3	4	5	6	7	8	9	10

4 4 4 4 4

4 + 0 = 4

3 + 1 = 4

2 + 2 = 4

1 + 3 = 4

1 + 3 = ☐	**0 + 4 =** ☐
2 + 2 = ☐	**3 + 1 =** ☐
4 + 0 = ☐	

4 is **1** more than ☐ and **1** less than ☐

Add 4. 

 add  equals **6**

$2 + 4 = 6$

+4

1	7
2	5
3	9
4	6
5	8

+4

1	→	5
2	→	
3	→	
4	→	
5	→	

↓ 4 4 4 4 4 4

4 4 4 4 4 4

Add.

● ●●●● ●●●●●

1 + 4 = 5 or $\begin{array}{r} 1 \\ +4 \\ \hline 5 \\ \hline \end{array}$

$\begin{array}{r} 0 \\ +4 \\ \hline \\ \hline \end{array}$ $\begin{array}{r} 1 \\ +4 \\ \hline \\ \hline \end{array}$ $\begin{array}{r} 2 \\ +4 \\ \hline \\ \hline \end{array}$ $\begin{array}{r} 3 \\ +4 \\ \hline \\ \hline \end{array}$

$\begin{array}{r} 4 \\ +4 \\ \hline \\ \hline \end{array}$ $\begin{array}{r} 5 \\ +4 \\ \hline \\ \hline \end{array}$ $\begin{array}{r} 6 \\ +4 \\ \hline \\ \hline \end{array}$ $\begin{array}{r} 4 \\ +0 \\ \hline \\ \hline \end{array}$

$\begin{array}{r} 4 \\ +1 \\ \hline \\ \hline \end{array}$ $\begin{array}{r} 4 \\ +2 \\ \hline \\ \hline \end{array}$

2 + 1 + 1 = ☐ 0 + 2 + 2 = ☐

1 + 2 + 1 = ☐ 4 + 0 + 0 = ☐

2 + 2 + 0 = ☐ 3 + 1 + 0 = ☐

1 + 1 + 1 + 1 = ☐ 0 + 1 + 3 = ☐

The story of **5**.

0	1	2	3	4	**5**	6	7	8	9	10

◆◆◆◆◆ + ☐ **5 + 0 = 5**

◆◆◆◆ + ◆ **4 + 1 = 5**

◆◆◆ + ◆◆ **3 + 2 = 5**

◆◆ + ◆◆◆ **2 + 3 = 5**

◆ + ◆◆◆◆ **1 + 4 = 5**

☐ + ◆◆◆◆◆ **0 + 5 = 5**

5 + 0 = ☐	**4 + 1 =** ☐
3 + 2 = ☐	**2 + 3 =** ☐
1 + 4 = ☐	**0 + 5 =** ☐

5 is **1** more than ☐ and **1** less than ☐

Add **5**. 

 add  equals **8**

3 + 5 = 8

+ 5

1	8
2	6
3	9
4	10
5	7

+ 5

1	→	6
2	→	
3	→	
4	→	
5	→	

5 5 5 5 5 5

5 5 5 5 5 5

Add.

● ●●●●● ●●●●●●

1 + 5 = 6 or $\begin{array}{r} 1 \\ +\,5 \\ \hline 6 \end{array}$

$\begin{array}{r} 0 \\ +\,5 \\ \hline \end{array}$ $\begin{array}{r} 1 \\ +\,5 \\ \hline \end{array}$ $\begin{array}{r} 2 \\ +\,5 \\ \hline \end{array}$ $\begin{array}{r} 3 \\ +\,5 \\ \hline \end{array}$

$\begin{array}{r} 4 \\ +\,5 \\ \hline \end{array}$ $\begin{array}{r} 5 \\ +\,5 \\ \hline \end{array}$ $\begin{array}{r} 5 \\ +\,1 \\ \hline \end{array}$ $\begin{array}{r} 5 \\ +\,0 \\ \hline \end{array}$

$\begin{array}{r} 5 \\ +\,2 \\ \hline \end{array}$ $\begin{array}{r} 5 \\ +\,3 \\ \hline \end{array}$

3 + 1 + 1 = ☐ 2 + 0 + 3 = ☐

2 + 1 + 2 = ☐ 5 + 0 + 0 = ☐

1 + 1 + 1 + 1 + 1 = ☐ 4 + 0 + 1 = ☐

0 + 3 + 2 = ☐ 1 + 1 + 3 = ☐

The story of 6.

0	1	2	3	4	5	**6**	7	8	9	10

6 + 0 = 6

5 + 1 = 6

4 + 2 = 6

3 + 3 = 6

2 + 4 = 6

1 + 5 = 6

0 + 6 = 6

6 6 6 6 6

3 + 3 = ☐	1 + 5 = ☐
5 + 1 = ☐	2 + 4 = ☐
6 + 0 = ☐	4 + 2 = ☐

6 is **1** more than ☐ and **1** less than ☐

Add **6** 

 add  equals **8**

2 + 6 = 8

+ 6

0	7
1	9
2	6
3	10
4	8

+ 6

0	→	6
1	→	
2	→	
3	→	
4	→	

6 6 6 6 6 6

6 6 6 6 6 6

Add.

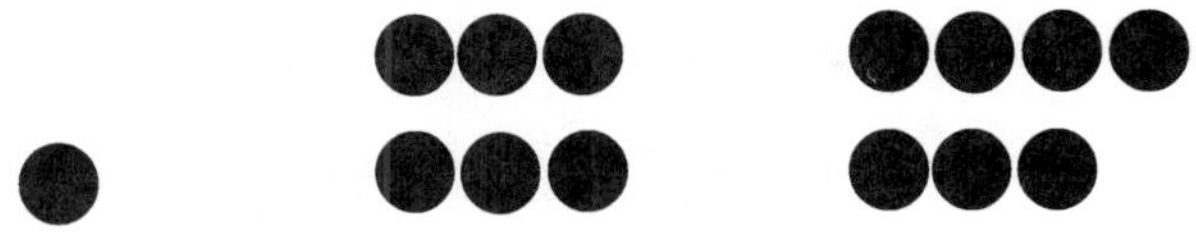

1 + 6 = 7 or $\begin{array}{r} 1 \\ +6 \\ \hline 7 \\ \hline \end{array}$

$\begin{array}{r} 0 \\ +6 \\ \hline \\ \hline \end{array}$ $\begin{array}{r} 1 \\ +6 \\ \hline \\ \hline \end{array}$ $\begin{array}{r} 2 \\ +6 \\ \hline \\ \hline \end{array}$ $\begin{array}{r} 3 \\ +6 \\ \hline \\ \hline \end{array}$

$\begin{array}{r} 4 \\ +6 \\ \hline \\ \hline \end{array}$ $\begin{array}{r} 6 \\ +0 \\ \hline \\ \hline \end{array}$ $\begin{array}{r} 6 \\ +1 \\ \hline \\ \hline \end{array}$ $\begin{array}{r} 6 \\ +2 \\ \hline \\ \hline \end{array}$

$\begin{array}{r} 6 \\ +3 \\ \hline \\ \hline \end{array}$ $\begin{array}{r} 6 \\ +4 \\ \hline \\ \hline \end{array}$

1 + 4 + 1 = ☐ 0 + 3 + 3 = ☐

2 + 2 + 2 = ☐ 3 + 1 + 2 = ☐

3 + 2 + 1 = ☐ 1 + 1 + 1 + 1 + 1 + 1 = ☐

5 + 0 + 1 = ☐ 0 + 4 + 2 = ☐

The story of **7**.

0	1	2	3	4	5	6	**7**	8	9	10

7 + 0 = 7

6 + 1 = 7

5 + 2 = 7

4 + 3 = 7

3 + 4 = 7

2 + 5 = 7

1 + 6 = 7

0 + 7 = 7

4 + 3 = ☐	0 + 7 = ☐
3 + 4 = ☐	6 + 1 = ☐
2 + 5 = ☐	7 + 0 = ☐
1 + 6 = ☐	5 + 2 = ☐

Add **7.** 

 add  equals **9**

2 + 7 = 9

+ 7

0	8
1	10
2	9
3	7

+ 7

0	→	7
1	→	
2	→	
3	→	

7 7 7 7 7 7

7 7 7 7 7 7

Add.

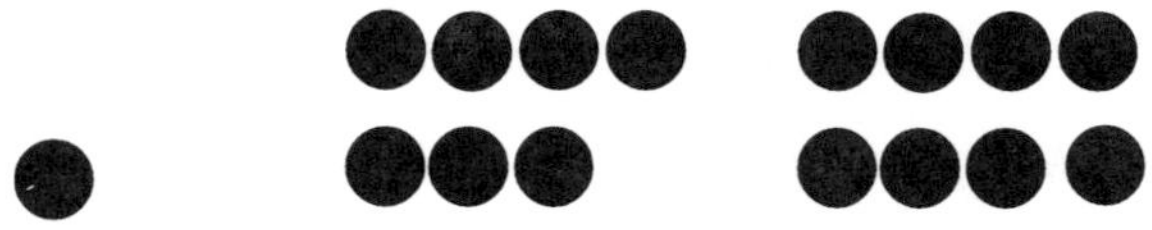

1 + 7 = 8 or

$$\begin{array}{r} 1 \\ +\,7 \\ \hline 8 \end{array}$$

$$\begin{array}{r} 0 \\ +\,7 \\ \hline \end{array} \qquad \begin{array}{r} 1 \\ +\,7 \\ \hline \end{array} \qquad \begin{array}{r} 2 \\ +\,7 \\ \hline \end{array} \qquad \begin{array}{r} 3 \\ +\,7 \\ \hline \end{array}$$

$$\begin{array}{r} 7 \\ +\,1 \\ \hline \end{array} \qquad \begin{array}{r} 7 \\ +\,0 \\ \hline \end{array} \qquad \begin{array}{r} 7 \\ +\,3 \\ \hline \end{array} \qquad \begin{array}{r} 7 \\ +\,2 \\ \hline \end{array}$$

$$\begin{array}{r} 7 \\ +\,4 \\ \hline \end{array} \qquad \begin{array}{r} 4 \\ +\,7 \\ \hline \end{array}$$

1+0+6= ☐ 2+2+3= ☐ 1+4+2= ☐

2+3+2= ☐ 5+1+1= ☐ 0+0+7= ☐

3+3+1= ☐ 5+2+0= ☐ 5+0+2= ☐

4+0+3= ☐ 6+0+1= ☐ 3+1+3= ☐

The story of 8.

0	1	2	3	4	5	6	7	**8**	9	10

$8 + 0 = 8$

$7 + 1 = 8$

$6 + 2 = 8$

$5 + 3 = 8$

$4 + 4 = 8$

$3 + 5 = 8$

$2 + 6 = 8$

$1 + 7 = 8$

$0 + 8 = 8$

$5 + 3 =$ ☐	$0 + 8 =$ ☐
$4 + 4 =$ ☐	$6 + 2 =$ ☐
$3 + 5 =$ ☐	$7 + 1 =$ ☐
$2 + 6 =$ ☐	$8 + 0 =$ ☐
$1 + 7 =$ ☐	

Add **8**. 

 add  equals **10**

2 + 8 = **10**

+ 8

0	9
1	10
2	8

+ 8

0	→	8

8 8 8 8 8 8

8 8 8 8 8 8

8 8 8 8 8 8

Add.

$1 + 8 = 9$ or

$$\begin{array}{r} 1 \\ +\,8 \\ \hline 9 \\ \hline \end{array}$$

$$\begin{array}{r} 0 \\ +\,8 \\ \hline \\ \hline \end{array} \quad \begin{array}{r} 1 \\ +\,8 \\ \hline \\ \hline \end{array} \quad \begin{array}{r} 2 \\ +\,8 \\ \hline \\ \hline \end{array} \quad \begin{array}{r} 8 \\ +\,1 \\ \hline \\ \hline \end{array}$$

$$\begin{array}{r} 8 \\ +\,0 \\ \hline \\ \hline \end{array} \quad \begin{array}{r} 8 \\ +\,2 \\ \hline \\ \hline \end{array} \quad \begin{array}{r} 7 \\ +\,3 \\ \hline \\ \hline \end{array} \quad \begin{array}{r} 7 \\ +\,2 \\ \hline \\ \hline \end{array}$$

$$\begin{array}{r} 7 \\ +\,1 \\ \hline \\ \hline \end{array} \quad \begin{array}{r} 7 \\ +\,0 \\ \hline \\ \hline \end{array}$$

5+1+2= ☐	1+6+1= ☐	2+2+2+2= ☐
6+1+1= ☐	2+4+2= ☐	3+3+1+1= ☐
7+1+0= ☐	3+1+4= ☐	4+0+2+2= ☐
8+0+0= ☐	5+3+0= ☐	1+2+0+5= ☐

The story of 9.

0	1	2	3	4	5	6	7	8	**9**	10

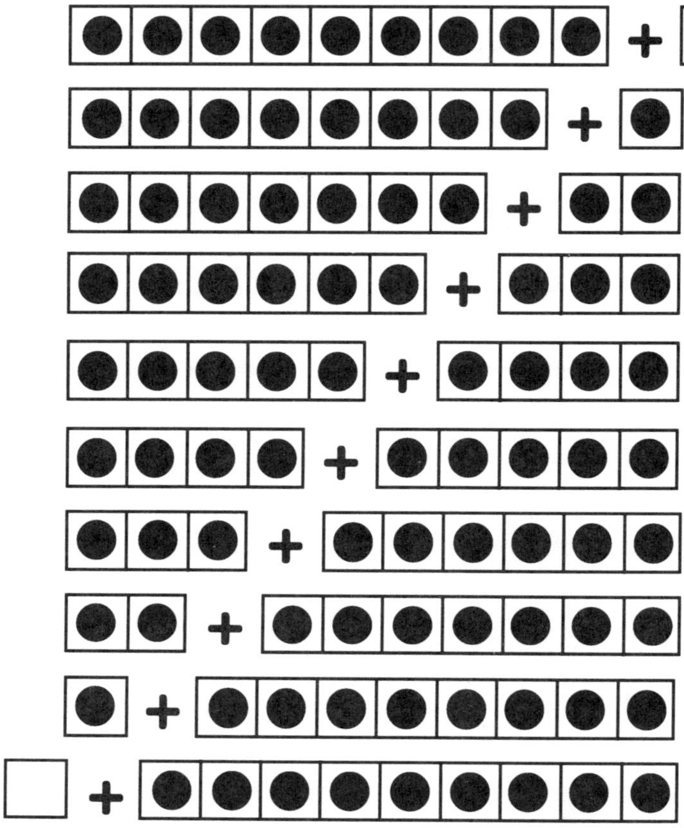

9+0=9

8+1=9

7+2=9

6+3=9

5+4=9

4+5=9

3+6=9

2+7=9

1+8=9

0+9=9

9

9

9

9

7 + 2 = ☐	6 + 3 = ☐
9 + 0 = ☐	8 + 1 = ☐
5 + 4 = ☐	7 + 2 = ☐
3 + 6 = ☐	1 + 8 = ☐
4 + 5 = ☐	0 + 9 = ☐

Add 9. 

 add 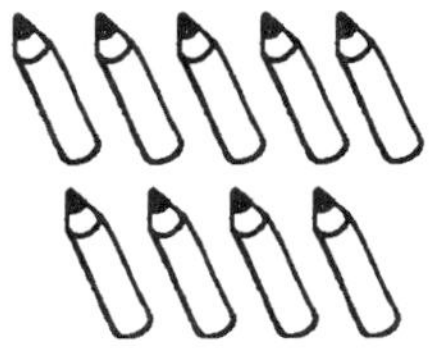 equals **10**

1 + 9 = **10**

+9

0	10
1	9

+9

0	→	
1	→	

9 9 9 9 9 9

9 9 9 9 9 9

9 9 9 9 9 9

Add.

$1 + 9 = 10$ or $\begin{array}{r} 1 \\ +\ 9 \\ \hline 10 \\ \hline \end{array}$

$\begin{array}{r} 9 \\ +\ 0 \\ \hline \\ \hline \end{array}$ $\begin{array}{r} 9 \\ +\ 1 \\ \hline \\ \hline \end{array}$ $\begin{array}{r} 0 \\ +\ 9 \\ \hline \\ \hline \end{array}$ $\begin{array}{r} 1 \\ +\ 9 \\ \hline \\ \hline \end{array}$

$\begin{array}{r} 8 \\ +\ 2 \\ \hline \\ \hline \end{array}$ $\begin{array}{r} 8 \\ +\ 1 \\ \hline \\ \hline \end{array}$ $\begin{array}{r} 8 \\ +\ 0 \\ \hline \\ \hline \end{array}$ $\begin{array}{r} 2 \\ +\ 8 \\ \hline \\ \hline \end{array}$

$\begin{array}{r} 1 \\ +\ 8 \\ \hline \\ \hline \end{array}$ $\begin{array}{r} 0 \\ +\ 8 \\ \hline \\ \hline \end{array}$

$4+4+1=\square$ $8+0+1=\square$ $2+1+6=\square$

$2+5+2=\square$ $1+7+1=\square$ $4+2+3=\square$

$6+1+2=\square$ $2+2+5=\square$ $6+0+3=\square$

The story of **10**.

0	1	2	3	4	5	6	7	8	9	**10**

10

10

10

10

10

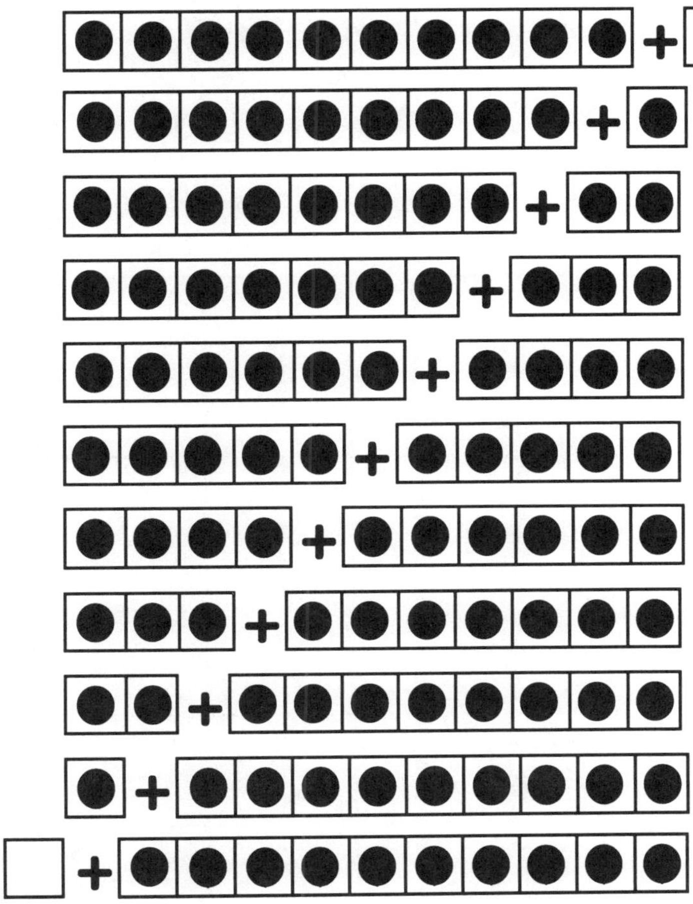

10+0=10

9+1=10

8+2=10

7+3=10

6+4=10

5+5=10

4+6=10

3+7=10

2+8=10

1+9=10

0+10=10

10 + 0 = ☐	3 + 7 = ☐
7 + 3 = ☐	9 + 1 = ☐
8 + 2 = ☐	5 + 5 = ☐
6 + 4 = ☐	0 + 10 = ☐

Add 0

add equals **10**

10 + 0 = **10**

+ 0

1	4
2	3
3	5
4	1
5	2
6	10
7	9
8	6
9	8
10	7

+ 0

1	→	1
2	→	
3	→	
4	→	
5	→	
6	→	
7	→	
8	→	
9	→	
10	→	

Add 1. 

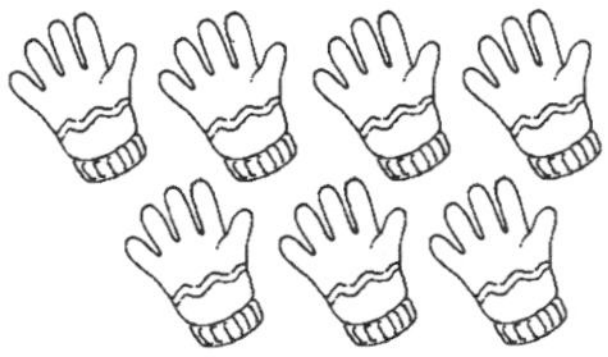 add  equals **8**

7 + 1 =

+1

1	5
2	2
3	6
4	3
5	4
6	9
7	10
8	8
9	7

+1

1	→	2
2	→	
3	→	
4	→	
5	→	
6	→	
7	→	
8	→	
9	→	

Fill in the missing numbers.

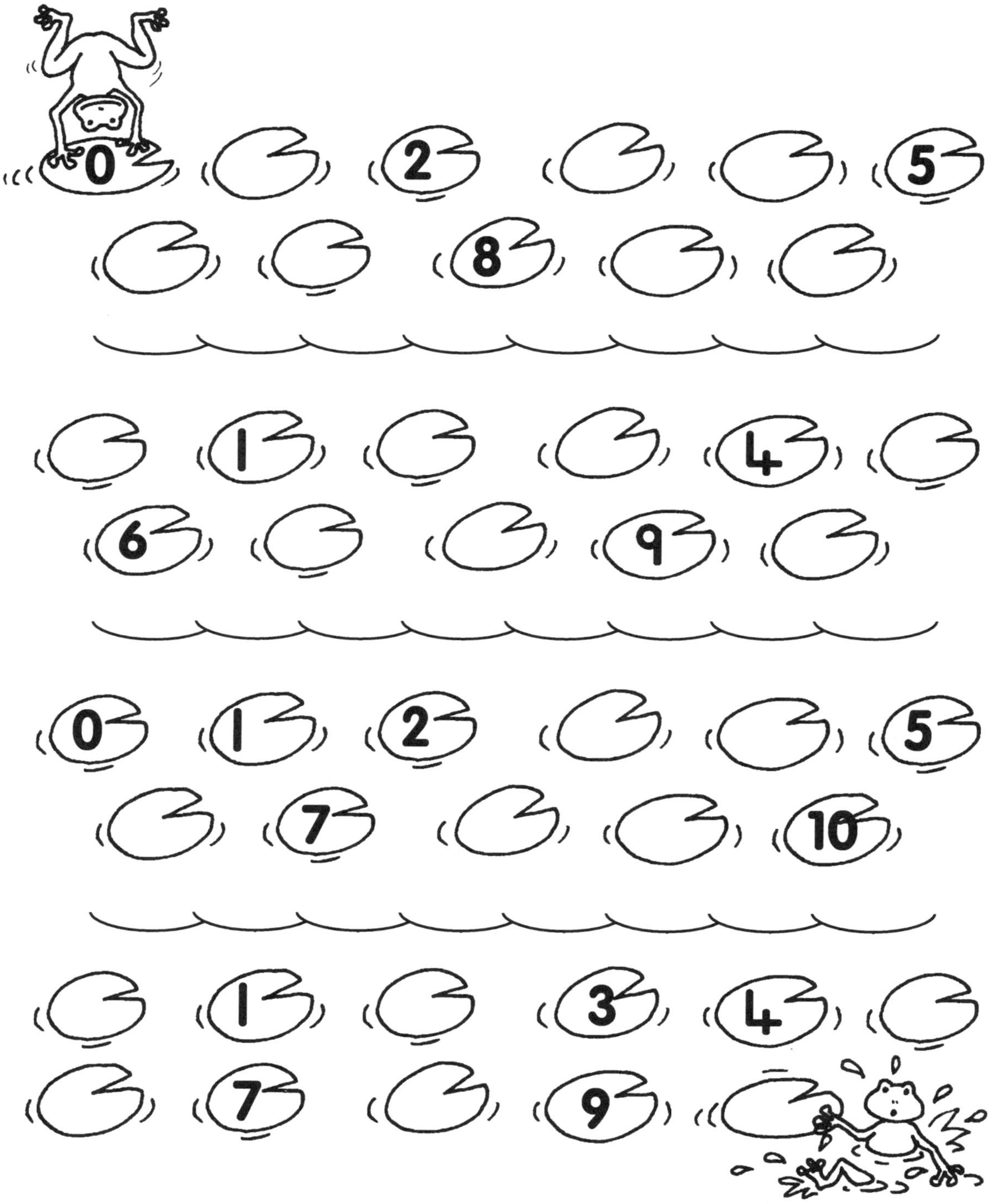

Add.

5 + 2	8 + 0	3 + 6	7 + 2
8 + 1	2 + 7	5 + 5	7 + 0
9 + 1	5 + 3	1 + 6	4 + 4
0 + 8	3 + 6	7 + 3	1 + 9
4 + 6	7 + 1	3 + 4	2 + 8

Add.

3	2	6	5
+ 4	+ 3	+ 2	+ 3
___	___	___	___
6	1	2	7
+ 4	+ 7	+ 4	+ 2
___	___	___	___
3	5	6	3
+ 2	+ 0	+ 3	+ 7
___	___	___	___
0	2	1	1
+ 10	+ 5	+ 3	+ 4
___	___	___	___
5	0	6	9
+ 5	+ 0	+ 1	+ 0
___	___	___	___

> means **more than.**

8 apples **5** oranges

Can you see **3 more** apples than oranges?

8
5

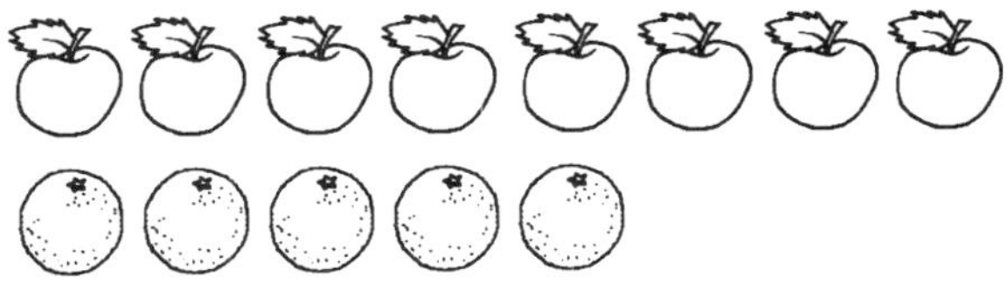

8 > 5

Colour and write how many more.

4 2		2	4>2
6 3			6>3
9 5			9>5
5 3			5>3
7 4			7>4
1 0			1>0

Who has **more**?

Rajan Eleanor

Colour 4 balloons in each hand.
There are **2** balloons left.
Rajan has **2 more** balloons.

6>4

Kio

Luke

Colour **2** cakes on each plate.
How many **more** cakes has Kio? ☐

3>2

Zoë

James

Colour **1** ball from each person.
How many **more** balls has Zoë? ☐

2>1

Helen

Juan

Colour **2** oranges on each plate.
How many **more** oranges has Helen? ☐

4>2

< means **less than.**

3 clubs

7 hearts

3 

7 

3 < 7

Write.

2 **4** 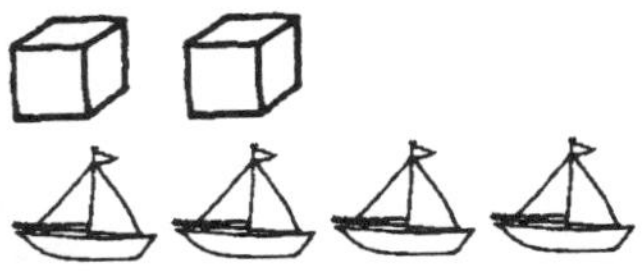	**2<4**
3 **6** 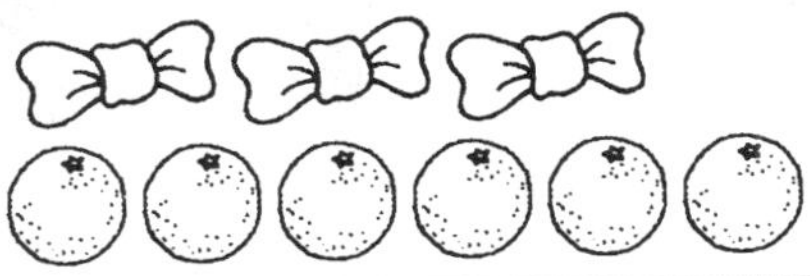	3<6
5 **9** 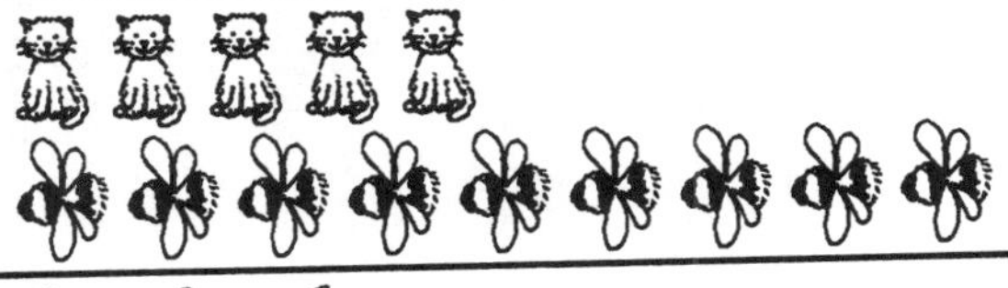	5<9
3 **5** 	3<5
4 **7** 	4<7
0 **1** 	0<1

Draw > or <

Remember

8 > 5　　5 < 8

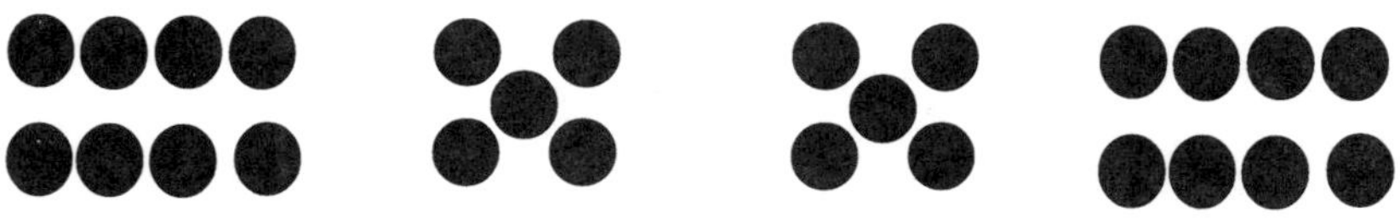

2 < 4	9 > 7	3 < 6
3 5	5 7	7 8
8 9	7 10	2 5
2 6	1 6	9 6
6 8	6 7	4 0
5 3	0 3	0 1
4 10	5 8	10 5

– meaning the difference between.

1	2	3	4		1	2	3

4 books **3** books

The difference between **4** and **3** is **1**.

4 – 3 = 1

Colour the ones left out to find the answer.

 **5 – 3 =** ☐	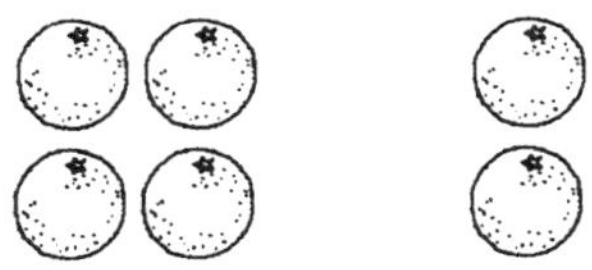 **4 – 2 =** ☐
 **3 – 1 =** ☐	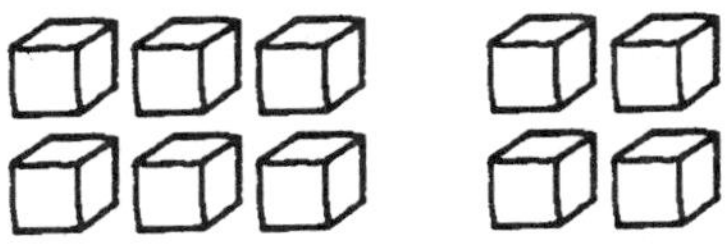 **6 – 4 =** ☐
 **7 – 3 =** ☐	 **4 – 1 =** ☐
 **2 – 1 =** ☐	 **6 – 6 =** ☐

Look and write.

zero	0	zero	0	+	1	=	1
one	1	one	1	+		=	2
two	2	two	2	+		=	3
three	3	three	3	+		=	4
four	4	four	4	+		=	5
five	5	five	5	+		=	6
six	6	six	6	+		=	7
seven	7	seven	7	+		=	8
eight	8	eight	8	+		=	9
nine	9	nine	9	+		=	10
ten	10	ten	10	+		=	10

Money.

Colour:

Brown	Brown	Grey	Grey	Grey
1p	2p	5p	10p	20p

 = p

 = p

 = p

Add

1p + 5p =

2p + 1p =

2p + 5p =

2p + 2p =

5p + 1p =

1p + 1p =

You can buy the same with this money.

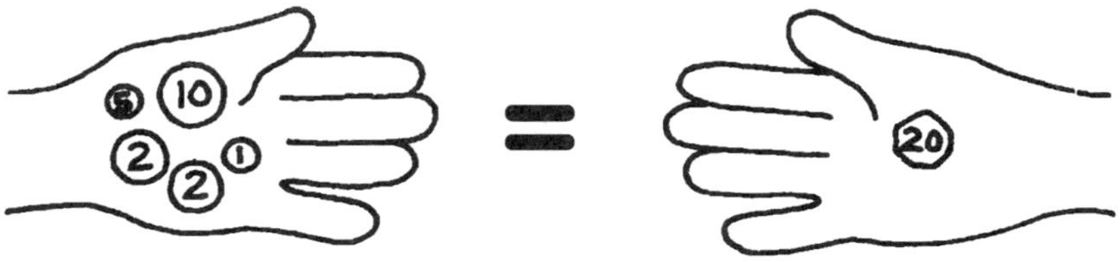

How much money?

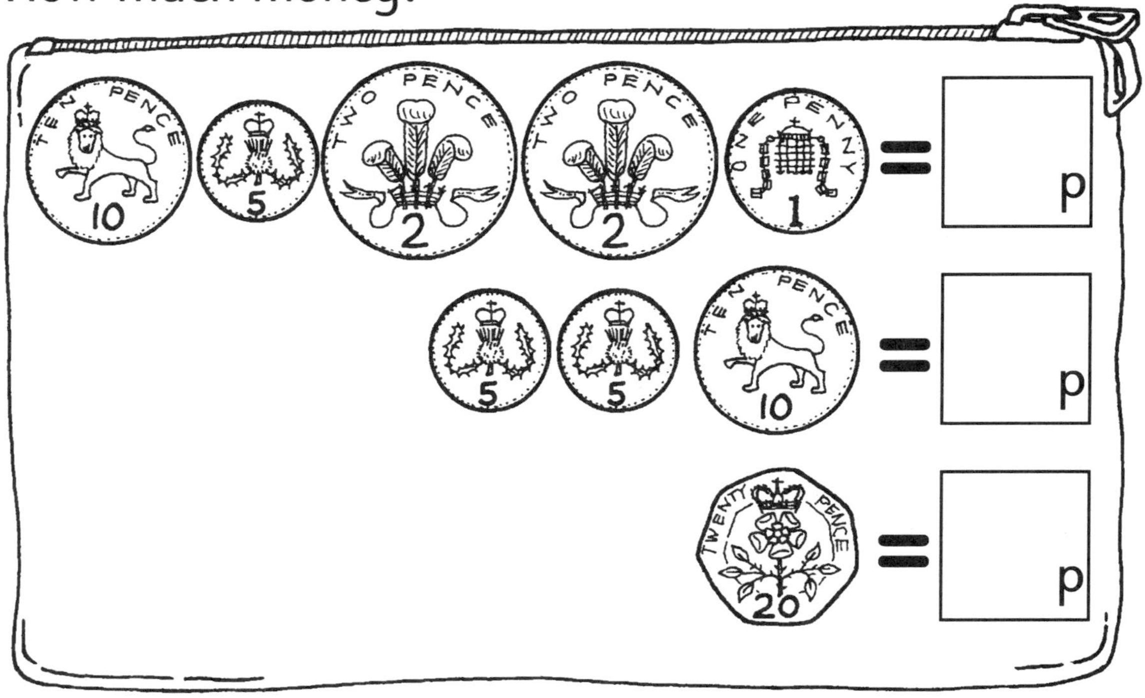

Add

10p + 5p + 2p + 2p + 1p = ☐

5p + 5p + 10p = ☐

1p + 2p + 5p + 2p = ☐

1p + 1p + 1p + 2p + 5p = ☐

Going shopping.

How much have you spent?

lollipop **2p**

sticker **5p**

sweet **1p**

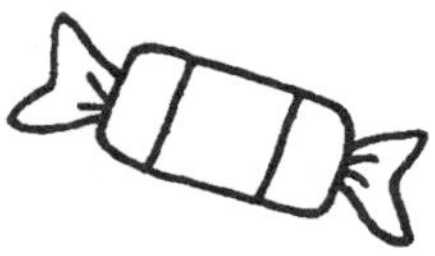

apple **5p**

1 sticker and
1 sweet ___ p

2 lollipops and
1 apple ___ p

2 sweets and
1 sticker ___ p

2 apples ___ p

1 lollipop and
3 sweets ___ p

2 stickers and
1 apple ___ p

Tens and units.

This is a ten.

It is made up of ten parts.

1	2	3	4	5	6	7	8	9	10

This is a unit. | 1 |

It is made up of one part.

Circle sets of ten. Count the units.

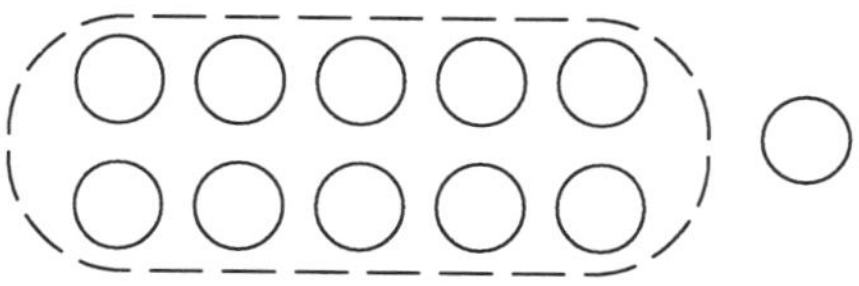	1	ten	1	unit
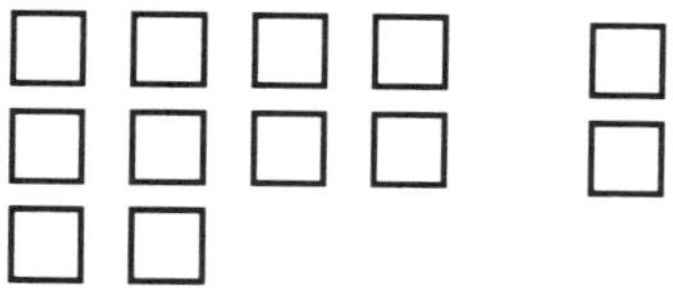		ten		units
		ten		units
		ten		units
		ten		units

Tens and units.

a ten

1	2	3	4	5	6	7	8	9	10

1	a unit

t stands for ten.
u stands for unit.

How many?

t, u — t u: 1 3	t, u — t u: 1 5
t, u — t u	t, u — t u
t, u — t u	t, u — t u
t — t u	t, u — t u

Tens and units.

1	2	3	4	5	6	7	8	9	10	11	12	13	14	15	16	17	18	19	20

Count tens and units on the number line.

Put your finger on **10**.
Count on **7** more.

10 + 7 =

t u

Put your finger on **10**.
Count on **4** more.

10 + 4 =

t u

Put your finger on **10**.
Count on **9** more.

10 + 9 =

t u

Put your finger on **10**.
Count on **8** more.

10 + 8 =

t u

Write the tens and units.

1 ten and **5** units.	t u
1 ten and **6** units.	t u
1 ten and **7** units.	t u
1 ten and **8** units.	t u
1 ten and **9** units.	t u
2 tens and **0** units.	t u

Add the tens and units.

t u	t u	t u
1 0	1 0	1 0
+ 2	+ 4	+ 6
____	____	____

t u	t u	t u
1 0	1 0	1 0
+ 1	+ 3	+ 5
____	____	____

t u	t u	t u
1 0	1 0	1 0
+ 9	+ 0	+ 1 0
____	____	____